The Kwame Nkrumah Cartoons
A VISUAL HISTORY OF THE TIMES

BABA G. JALLOW

WOELI PUBLISHING SERVICES
ACCRA
2014

Published by
Woeli Publishing Services
P. O. Box NT 601
Accra New Town
Ghana
Tel.: 0289535570
Email: woeli@woelipublishing.com
woeli@libr.ug.edu.gh
Website: www.woelipublishing.com

© Baba G. Jallow, 2014
ISBN 978-9964-90-261-1
ALL RIGHTS RESERVED
Typeset by Woeli Publishing Services, Accra

Contents

INTRODUCTION   v

PART I

PRE-COUP CARTOONS
(1961–1966)   1

PART II

POST-COUP CARTOONS
(1966–ONWARD)   59

Introduction

After a twelve-year sojourn in the United States and Britain, Kwame Nkrumah returned to the Gold Coast in 1947 at the invitation of the United Gold Coast Convention (UGCC). The UGCC leadership needed someone who had the time, the energy and the skills to serve as Secretary General of the first major political party in the country Gold Coast (now Ghana). Nkrumah seemed a perfect fit. During the twelve years he spent abroad, Nkrumah was engaged in study and political activism. In the United States, he studied at Lincoln University, where he obtained a Bachelor of Arts degree in Sociology and Economics in 1939 and a Bachelor of Theology degree in 1942. He also obtained a Master of Science degree in Education as well as a Master of Arts degree in Philosophy from the University of Pennsylvania in 1942 and 1943, respectively. When he migrated to Britain in 1943, he got involved in the emergent pan-African movement and was an active member of London-based nationalist groups. It was while in London that his knack for organization and activism caught the attention of Dr. J. B. Danquah and the leadership of the UGCC, who invited him and paid his way back home to become secretary general of their new party. In 1949, less than two years after he returned home, Nkrumah broke with the UGCC and launched his own party, the Convention People's Party (CCP), which led the country to internal self-government in 1951 and independence in 1957.

Even before accepting the invitation to return to the Gold Coast and work for the UGCC, Nkrumah knew that his association with that party was doomed to failure. He knew that Dr. J. B. Danquah and the rest of the UGCC leadership were dedicated exponents of the capitalist worldview. J. B. Danquah was a wealthy lawyer and the UGCC was funded by the even wealthier merchant, J. B. Grant. Nkrumah, a fanatic admirer of socialist doctrine, admits in his autobiography that when he received their invitation, he knew "it was quite useless to associate myself with a movement backed almost entirely by reactionaries, middle class lawyers, and merchants, for my revolutionary background and ideas would make it impossible for me to work with them" (Nkrumah 1957: 62). He admits that he had his own plans and would not hesitate to pursue them whether the UGCC leadership liked it or not (Nkrumah 1957).

Nkrumah knew that the UGCC's gradualist approach to anticolonial nationalism was incompatible with his own radical approach to the colonial question. The UGCC wanted self-government "within the shortest possible time." While the UGCC differed from earlier nationalist groups like the Aborigine's Rights Protection Society and the National Congress of British West Africa in that it sought independence as opposed to mere Africanization of the colonial bureaucracy, it was prepared to exercise some patience in pursuit of that objective. Nkrumah, on the other hand, wanted "self-government now" under the leadership of a revolutionary vanguard party and a socialist people's parliament. The two approaches represented opposing and conflicting visions of how and when Ghana should become independent. They proved totally irreconcilable; the battle between them was to the death.

Nkrumah's vision of Ghana as a socialist republic which would serve as the center for pan-African unification and the fight against imperialism and neocolonialism drove his domestic policy choices and actions. His fatal political flaw was that within the context of that vision, Nkrumah saw no need for alternative political parties espousing contending visions of nation statehood. In other words, he opted for a regime of coercion that monopolized the right to define what Ghana was and what Ghana would become. His government passed a series of repressive laws — including the notorious Preventive Detention Act of 1958 — to muzzle all criticism of his policies and all opposition to his government. He turned Ghana into a republic in 1960, was declared Life President in 1963, and made Ghana a single-party state in 1964. Two years later on February 24, 1966, he was forcibly removed from power in a military-police coup while on a trip to Vietnam at the invitation of Ho Chi Minh. The coup- makers established the National Liberation Council that oversaw a three-year transition period which culminated in the election of Dr. Kofi Busia as Prime Minister of the short-lived Second Republic. Nkrumah spent the rest of his days in neighbouring Guinea, where his friend, President Sekou Toure named him honourary co-president. He died in a Rumanian hospital in April 1972. After a lengthy string of negotiations between Sekou Toure and a succession of Ghanaian governments, Nkrumah's remains were eventually returned to Ghana.

Nkrumah's immediate political legacy was a quarter century of civic crises in Ghana. Between 1966 when he was overthrown and the inauguration of the Fourth Republic in 1993, Ghana had six different governments, four military and two civilian: the National Liberation Council (1966–1969), the Second Republic (1969–1972), the National Redemption Council/Supreme Military Council I & II (1972–1979), the Armed Forces Revolutionary Council (1979), the Third Republic (1979–1981), and the Provisional National Defense Council (1981–1992). Ghana has moved a long way away from the culture of political intolerance created by Nkrumah and perpetuated by the SMC and PNDC governments. It took massive civil society action by such groups as the Movement for Peace and Justice, the Association of Recognized Professional Bodies, the Front for the Prevention of Dictatorship, the Ghana Bar Association and the Ghana Christian Council, among others, to force a return to multi-party democratic politics and the inauguration of the Fourth Republic in 1993.

However, Nkrumah did great things for Ghana and for Africa. Woeli Dekutsey (2012) reports that Nkrumah "established 52 state enterprises, including 25 manufacturing and industrial enterprises . . ., instituted a free education and a free textbook scheme" and built two state universities in addition to the University of Ghana at Legon. He also granted scholarships to students from other parts of Africa to study at Ghanaian institutions of higher learning. "To give a boost to Black Studies," he "established the Institute of African Studies on the campus of the University of Ghana, Legon . . . On the sea, Ghana was sailing its own fleet of ships under the Black Star Line brand. In the sky, Ghana was flying its own airline, Ghana Airways" (Dekutsey 2012: 36). He was instrumental in the formation of the Organization of African Unity (now African Union) in 1963 and did a lot for the cause of pan-Africanism and decolonization.

Nevertheless, when he was overthrown, Ghanaians "vented their anger on an inanimate statue of Nkrumah and broke its neck and arm. To this day, this statue stands forlorn in the forecourt of the National Museum, with its headless body and broken arm, a symbol of Nkrumah's broken and decapitated dreams" (Dekutsey 2012: 43). A structure depicting Nkrumah's broken dreams stands behind his full statue at the Nkrumah mausoleum in Accra, this time in the form of "a marble figure of a tree with only the stump showing, as if its growth has been cut out too soon" (Dekutsey 2012: 49).

Cartoon-Speak in Ghana: Before and After Nkrumah

Regular cartoons often reflect dissenting opinion, a degree of public anger or a spirit of activism against any number of perceived social ills. They are a form of "angry laughter" indulged at the expense of the perceived perpetrators of "social ills." They are often on the side of the underdog and could potentially be subversive of authority, secular, religious or otherwise. They feed on the art of gross exaggeration and deliver their punches by gross magnification or diminution of their subject. Often, over a period of time, cartoons evolve into sophisticated narratives on historical events and representations of historical realities. This book represents one such cartoon narrative.

Nkrumah was a constant presence on the editorial cartoon pages of the *Accra Evening News*, the official mouthpiece of his party, the CPP. However, it was interesting to note that while Nkrumah was depicted as a hero and a saint in the pre-coup cartoons, he was depicted as a villain and a devil in the post-coup cartoons. While in power, journalists at the *Accra Evening News* loudly sang Nkrumah's praises, comparing him to Christ, Muhammad and the Buddha. These same journalists authored highly uncomplimentary, even insulting images of Nkrumah after his fall from power.

Cartoon depictions of Nkrumah as a hero, a saviour and a saint literally died with his regime. Overnight, he became a devil who, it was suggested by the cartoonists, during all his years in power thrived on the blood and sweat of Ghanaians. If these allegations were right, why did they portray Nkrumah in highly flattering terms while he was in power? And what are the implications of this representational transformation from highly hagiographic depictions of the Ghanaian leader before the coup to highly critical lampoons after the coup for our understanding of the historical Nkrumah and the nature of historical knowledge and evidence? A desire to probe these questions was a key motivation for the collection and publication of this book on Nkrumah cartoons.

The Nkrumah cartoons might loosely be divided into six interconnected categories. The first three of these are found in pre-coup editions of the *Evening News*, covering the period 1961 to

February 1966.* The second and third categories cover the post-February 24, 1966 coup. Two other categories, depicting Ghana itself and Nkrumah's party, the CPP, are found in both the pre-coup and post-coup cartoons. All cartoons undergo a pictorial and representational transformation as the narrative moves past February 24, 1966.

The first category of pre-coup cartoons comment on major international issues of Nkrumah's day: A 1961 cartoon depicts Britain as a fat, old, balding man on his knees beside a bed and before an image of the devil on the opposite wall praying "... And please God don't let the UN Committee go into South West Africa..."; another cartoon shows Tunisia and Algeria exploding into the face of France; a third shows Portugal whipping Britain for carrying Angola on her back. Other international issues reflected in this category include the North Atlantic Treaty Organization (NATO), the United States, Ghana-Togo relations, Apartheid South Africa, and the British dilemma whether to join the European Common Market or stay with the Commonwealth. The crisis in Southern Rhodesia (now Zimbabwe) over Ian Smith's Unilateral Declaration of Independence features prominently. Done by the cartoonists Thiks, Ghanatta, Kweku and Samco, these international cartoons are similar in that they all speak the language of Nkrumahism: They are all condemnations of imperialism, neo-colonialism, and their perceived instruments and stooges in Africa and abroad as articulated by Nkrumah. They are all appendices to the official narrative of the Nkrumah government on international issues. They were held to reflect "popular" sentiment which was supposed to mirror

---

* For the past three years, an increasing number of Ghanaian newspapers at the Ghana National Archives in Accra have become inaccessible to researchers. They are all said to be taken out of circulation for repair. One hopes that PRAAD is given the support required to salvage these important repositories of Ghanaian history.

official Ghana policy. Nkrumah loyalists were of the kind that unquestionably obeyed the leader in all cases and were ready to pounce on his perceived opponents and critics over every issue. The *Evening News* of Nkrumah's day was literally a shouting forum against perceived enemies, real or imagined.

A second category of pre-coup cartoons depict Nkrumah's political opponents. These images became especially prominent in the wake of a series of bomb explosions at Kulungugu and Accra, allegedly carried out by opposition elements of the United Party/National Liberation Movement, most of them former colleagues of Nkrumah in the CPP and the United Gold Coast Convention (UGCC). Following the promulgation of the Preventive Detention Act in 1958, many opposition leaders were detained, some fled into exile and some, like J. B. Danquah, Obetsebi Lamptey, Kofi Busia, Tawiah Adamafio and Komla Gbedemah were implicated in alleged conspiracies against Nkrumah's life. These "enemies of progress" are depicted in this category of cartoons as horned devils and rats, shady characters, enemies of Ghana working with external imperialists and neocolonialists to disrupt Nkrumah's "great programme on Work and Happiness for all." One cartoon depicts sacked Chief Justice Sir Arku Korsah assailed in a nightmare by the angry ghosts of innocent bomb blast victims. Sir Arku Korsah was sacked after he acquitted former Nkrumah associates accused of involvement in plots against Nkrumah's life. Korsah's replacement duly found the accused persons guilty and handed down sentences.

A third category of cartoons depicts Nkrumah himself. Found exclusively in the pre-coup pages of the *Evening News*, these are not cartoons in the normal sense of the term. They are the direct obverse of the cartoon as critique. They are not inspired by the anger or activism that animates classical cartoons. They are in fact songs in praise of The Leader, highly inflated hagiographies and adulations of Kwame Nkrumah that almost deify him: One cartoon shows him as Christ on a pedestal, surrounded by a circle of light, his right arm raised in blessing as the crowds below wondered at the unbelievable glory. One man in the crowd says, "Where am I? In Jericho, London or Utopia?" Another retorts: "Are you a stranger here? Rip-Van-Winkle! This is Ghana which Nkrumah founded." A particularly interesting cartoon depicts a broadly smiling Nkrumah, draped in traditional Ghanaian attire and holding a little lamb. Below it the cartoonist comments: "Osagyefo, the Good Shepherd. The Nation's Fount of Honour." In other cartoons, Nkrumah is depicted variously as "Hero of African redemption," "Africa's Man of Destiny," "Our Liberator, Teacher, Guardian and Leader," "The Apostle of African Freedom and Unity," among many other flattering titles and representations. One especially interesting cartoon shows Nkrumah glittering in the sky as "The Star of Africa." Nkrumah is also shown cheerfully leading a group of African leaders — including a delighted Jomo Kenyatta and his signature fly whisk — towards eventual African unity. Other cartoons show him leading large crowds of Africans towards liberation or in the relentless charge against imperialism, colonialism and neo-colonialism; or, as "Worker Number One," leading a crowd of workers on the march towards "Work and Happiness for All."

The last favourable depiction of Nkrumah in the pre-coup *Evening News* was a Monday, February 21, 1966 front page shot of the Ghanaian leader broadly smiling and waving a small handkerchief. The lead caption read, "THE LEADER LEAVES FOR HANOI." The short story reports that Nkrumah left for Hanoi that morning on a friendly visit to the Republic of North Vietnam at the invitation of President Ho Chi Minh. The story also reports what was most certainly the last major act Nkrumah performed as head of state: that he had set up a three-man Presidential Commission to run the country in his absence. An "executive instrument published in Accra" that morning named the members of the Presidential Commission as "Nana Freku the third, President of the Western Region House of Chiefs, Mr. N. A. Welbeck, Minister of State for Party Propaganda and Opanyin Kwame Poku, National President, United Ghana Farmer's Cooperative Council." The composition of the commission perhaps raised some eyebrows in Ghana, but few anticipated that three days later, a combined police-military coup dubbed "Operation Cold Chop" would topple the Nkrumah regime. News of his overthrow reached Nkrumah on a stopover in Peking, China while en route to Vietnam.

In the March 1 issue of the *Evening News*, Nkrumah is depicted by the cartoonist Ghanatta as "Nkrumah — The Vicious Octopus," his tentacles firmly wrapped around basic commodities: liberty, democracy, justice, wealth, confidence, free voting, and free expression; a near-naked Ghana stands bound hand and feet in a corner lamenting, "Oh, my possessions." In the next issue, Nkrumah is depicted as a giant scaled snake with dragon claws tightly wrapped around a screaming Ghana. In the March 4 issue, Nkrumah is depicted as a giant rat greedily perched on the "remains of Ghana's wealth" as Ghana sat tightly bound and blindfolded on a nearby chair. On another page of the same issue, Nkrumah is depicted as *Sasa Bonsam*, an Akan variation for the devil. Yet another cartoon depicts Nkrumah as a naked devil, a rope around his waist held by a soldier leading a crowd of men, women and children chasing him as he tried to escape with State Funds. He is also depicted in this category as a naked devil worshipper, a disciple of *Kankan Nyame* and a playboy gleefully handing over bags of cash to his alleged numerous girlfriends. In one particularly telling cartoon titled, "NKRUMAH HAS FALLEN FROM GRACE TO GRASS LIKE NEBUCHADNEZZAR," Ghanatta depicts the fallen Ghanaian leader as a hairy creature on all fours with a branch clenched between his front teeth. Another cartoon shows him arriving in tears at Conakry Airport and

Sekou Toure consoling him with the words, "Don't worry, I will make you president of Guinea." Was Nkrumah actually in tears when he landed in Conakry from China? Or was the cartoon intended as mere mockery? To what extent does the cartoon narrative seek to approximate historical reality? And might a cartoon of this sort help but reflect a version of historical reality, however skewed? All cartoons in this category were done by Ghanatta, a cartoonist who authored some of the most hagiographic of the pre-coup depictions of Kwame Nkrumah. Ghanatta appears to have been the *Evening News'* "editorial cartoonist" in the months leading up to and immediately after the coup. What Ghanatta *really* thought of Nkrumah is impossible to tell from his work.

Also found exclusively in the post-coup period is another category of cartoons depicting Nkrumah's former associates. While the pre-coup hagiographic cartoons rarely, if ever, featured a minister or some other important person in the Nkrumah party-government, the post-coup cartoon narrative is crowded by key associates of the former president. The former "minions" of "The Chosen One" now joined him in the visual mud. Among many former Nkrumah associates depicted in this category are N. A. Welbeck, Kwaw Swanzy, Isaac Amihere, Kofi Baako, Tachie Menson, Krobo Edusei, and Ayeh Kumi. They are all depicted as corrupt and willing stooges of Kwame Nkrumah, some on the run, some begging for mercy, some dressed as women trying to escape, some hiding under the bed, some walking out of prison only to be slapped with "further charges." However, the satiric depictions of his former associates come nowhere near the ugly light in which Nkrumah himself is rendered after February 24, 1966.

The dramatic change of cartoon narratives from highly inflated hagiographies on Nkrumah before he was overthrown to the extremely harsh depictions of the same man after the coup raises some profound questions on the nature of historical knowledge, on the workings of power, and on people's incredible capacity to trade allegiances or say what they do not mean. Considering the alleged social construction of reality, the shift in the cartoon narrative after February 24, 1966 raises interesting questions over just what to make of Nkrumah's historical reality. Was the *faultless* Nkrumah of the pre-coup days really the *evil* Nkrumah of the post-coup days? If so, why was the evil Nkrumah of the post-coup days not depicted in the pre-coup cartoons? If not, why would Ghanatta, a cartoonist who rendered Nkrumah in such glowing terms before the coup suddenly depict him in the worst possible light after the coup? Why could we not ever tell, from the historical evidence, what Ghanatta really thought of Nkrumah? And into what light, or darkness does this question throw the concept of historical knowledge? Are we all just acting out roles rather than our real self as Lacan might suggest? In one pre-coup cartoon, Ghanatta depicts Nkrumah as the "Rock of Ages" and comments, "Go ahead Nkrumah, we support you." In a post-coup cartoon, Ghanatta shows Nkrumah gleefully handing over bags of hundreds of thousands of pounds sterling to a ring of fashionable ladies and comments, "Nkrumah's extravagant gifts to his many girlfriends earned him the title 'Show-Boy'." Since Show Boy was one of Nkrumah's earliest titles, Ghanatta suggests that he knew of his extravagant gifts to fashionable ladies for a long time, since the early fifties at least, when Nkrumah was prime minister. Might a need for survival warrant such enduring suppression of true emotion in favour of fictional adulation of the disliked? It is questions of this nature that readers are invited to contemplate as they browse through *The Kwame Nkrumah Cartoons*.

A chapter in Achille Mbembe's *On the Postcolony* titled, "The Thing and Its Doubles" examines the extent to which political cartoons satirizing Cameroonian president Paul Biya are a true, if not obvious reflections of his actual personality. The cartoons studied by Mbembe are of the classical satirical type, similar to the post-coup depictions of Nkrumah in Ghana. Their main difference with the Nkrumah cartoons is that they depicted a sitting president in unfavourable light, right under his nose. Such a scenario was impossible in Nkrumah's Ghana both because it would have been drastically punished the first time and because by 1961 when our narrative starts, all newspapers were state-owned and could only sing the praises of the government. It would be simplistic to suggest that all newspaper journalists in an all-state-owned media environment are sycophants. But if they must express themselves, they had to do so in terms complimentary to the state, one way or another. They cannot express views critical of the government, if for the mere fact that the editor will not publish them since they could find themselves without a job and behind bars in a minute. In Nkrumah's Ghana, such a "crime" was punishable by preventive detention under the PDA.

Much like the Biya cartoons, *The Kwame Nkrumah Cartoons* contributes to a tradition of the visual narrative of the political, which is to say, — the everyday, in contemporary society. The Nkrumah cartoons suggest that this tradition is complicated when the subject expresses other than it believes.

This book is divided into two sections. The first section covers cartoons produced before the 24 February 1966 coup; and the second section covers cartoons produced after the coup. Within these two sections, the individual cartoons themselves are not arranged in any particular order. This is because we want each section to represent a nuanced narrative on representations of Nkrumah, his supporters, his critics and the wider world within which they lived and operated. While dates are important in historical narratives, the aim of this book is to compare and contrast representations of the Ghanaian leader and other aspects of Ghanaian, African and world history during Nkrumah's last years in power and immediately after his removal from power; to compare and contrast depictions of Nkrumah at the height of his power with depictions of Nkrumah after he was no longer in power. The pre-coup and post-coup periods are presented as distinct but overlapping historical spaces. The reader is encouraged to observe what changed in Ghana after 24 February 1966 and what remained the same after that fateful date, and why. While answers to this question are inherent in the cartoon narrative presented in this book, they are also inherent in the nature of politics, power and the human condition itself.

BABA G. JALLOW

PART I

Pre-Coup Cartoons
(1961–1966)

Hero of African redemption

The above portrait of Osagyefo Dr Kwame Nkrumah, reveals the deep wisdom of the champion of champions in the African struggle against imperialism. Ghana is indeed fortunate to have such a man as Founder of the Nation.

IN this battle-field of life
   Where imperialism flounders,
Osagyefo of Ghana show thy light!
For the peoples of Africa to follow.

In the darkness of this age
When selfish man the way sees not,
Osagyefo of Ghana show thy light!
For the peoples of Africa to follow.

In the whirligig of time
When joy or sorrow is man's lot,
Osagyefo of Ghana show thy light!
For the peoples of Africa to follow

When Imperialists deny
Full Human Rights to suff'ring States,
Osagyefo of Ghana show thy light!
For the peoples of Africa to follow

While the East and West compete
For modern weapons man to kill,
Osagyefo of Ghana show thy light!
For the peoples of Africa to follow

When the Leaders of this world
Confer to find the Way to peace,
Osagyefo of Ghana show thy light!
For the peoples of Africa to follow.

In the midst of trusted friends
Where flatt'ry marks each smiling face,
Osagyefo of Ghana show thy light!
For the peoples of Africa to follow

At the Kulungugu thorp
Where hidden lay the mortal bomb,
Osagyefo of Ghana show thy light!
For the peoples of Africa to follow.

In the thick of cruel plots
While Chiefs and people stand by thee,
Osagyefo of Ghana show thy light!
For the peoples of Africa to follow

At the gate of Flagstaff House
Where hatred eyed the surging crowd,
Osagyefo of Ghana show thy light!
For the peoples of Africa to follow.

In the hour of curfew night
When silence reigns O'er all Accra,
Osagyefo of Ghana show thy light!
For the peoples of Africa to follow.

By his courageous device—
This "Work for Health and Happiness"
Osagyefo has truly shown the way
Which the peoples of Africa should follow!

Long live Osagyefo!
Long live the people's Leader!
Long live the Light of Africa.

              J. ABEDI-BOAFO
            DISTRICT COMMISSIONER

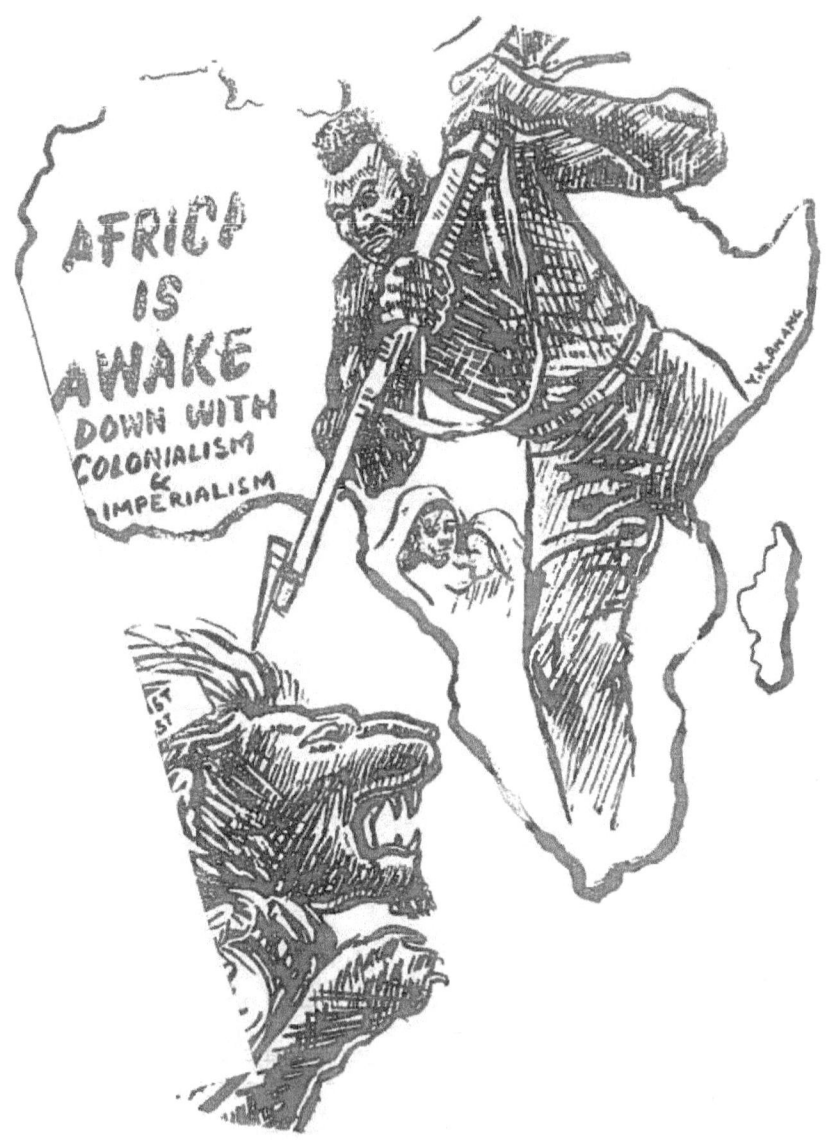

OSAGYEFO, THE LIBERATOR

THIS is the man!...the dreamer!
The visionary!...the missioner!-
The great liberator!
How intense!...how impressive,
How dramatic, grand and positive,
Those curves and lines so vital,
Exquisitely spiritual! . . .
The artist caught him right,
In a fine stream of light,
That tells the world that Africa shall rise.
The message flashes in his dark-brown eyes!

This is the man!.. the Leader!—
The great emancipator,
Nkrumah of Africa!...
There's something all-compelling,
In that portrait that's all-telling,
A message of liberation,
And Africa's salvation!—

REVIVAL bells are ringing over Africa's verdant sod. Come ye faithful ones, gather round our mighty Union tree.

Pre-coup Cartoons

Pre-coup Cartoons

AFRICA TRIUMPHS UNDER ITS FORCE, ITS BLAZE

A REVOLUTIONARY, CONTINENTAL PHILOSOPHY PUTS IMPERIALISM TO ROUT !

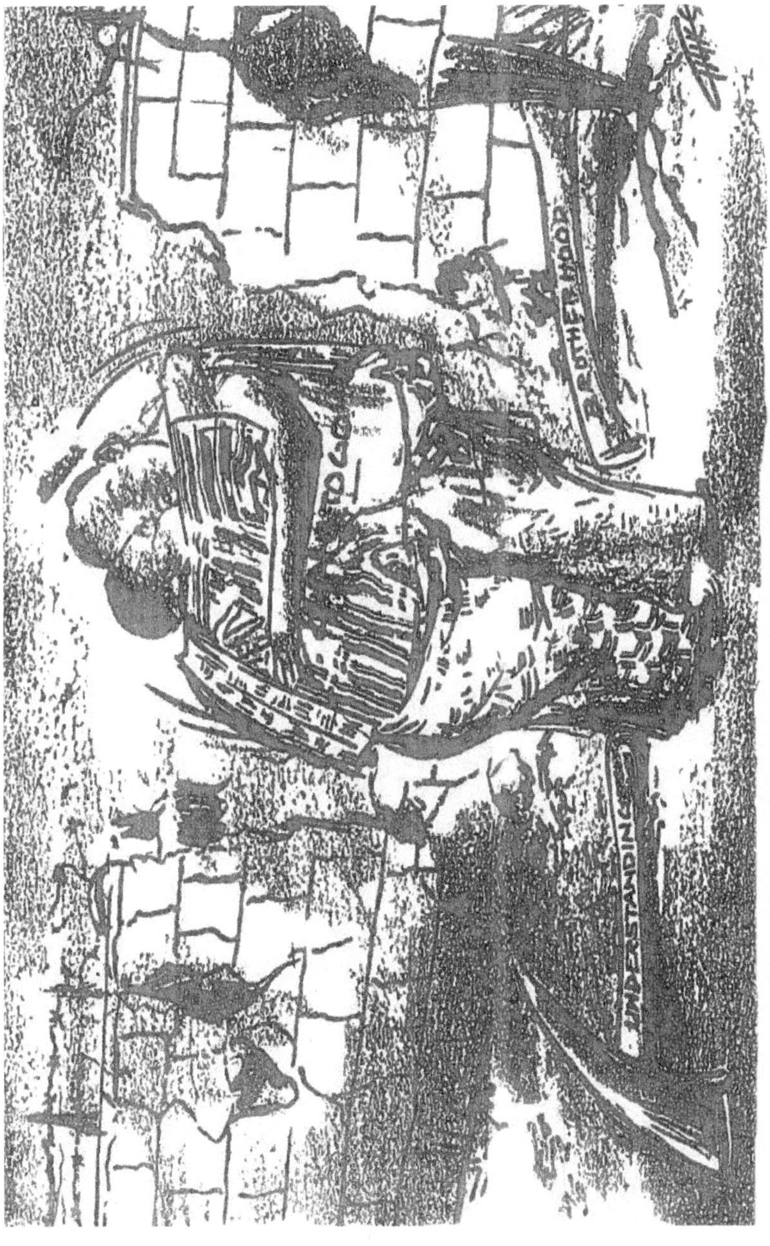

Pre-coup Cartoons

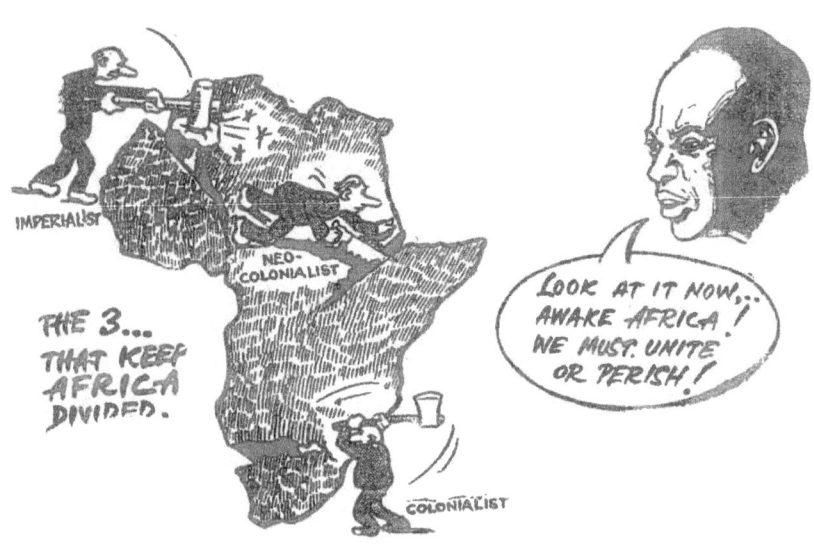

Pre-coup Cartoons

Osagyefo radiating the power behind Nkrumaism

Pre-coup Cartoons

OSAGYEFO rushes on killer — blocks with his right hand — grabs killer's wrist holding rifle.

OSAGYEFO holds killer's right wrist tightly — OSAGYEFO turns quick and swings killer over his back — causing killer to lose hold on rifle.

OSAGYEFO thrusts killer to ground — pins him down — forcing killer to surrender.

Pre-coup Cartoons

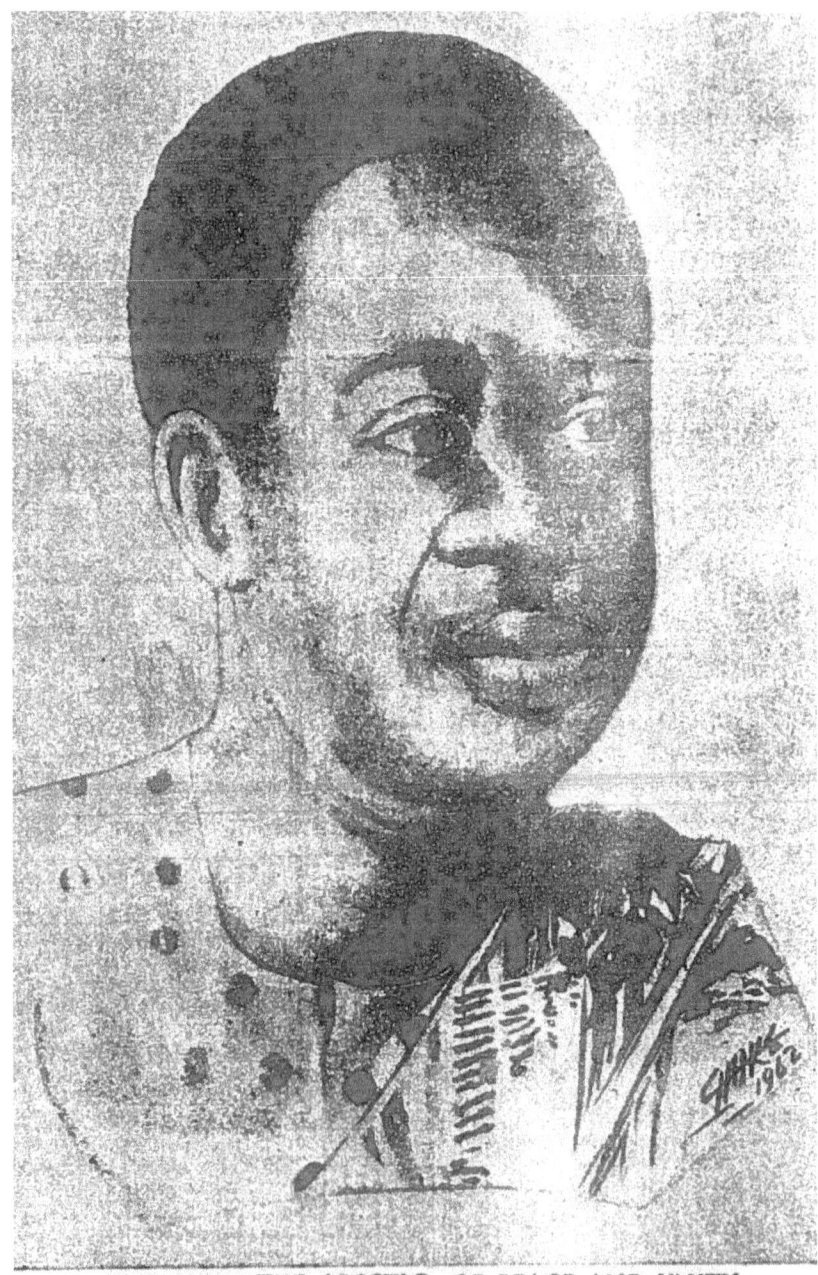

OSAGYEFO—THE APOSTLE OF PEACE AND UNITY

PART II

Post-Coup Cartoons
(1966–ONWARD)

DOWNFALL OF A DICTATOR!

'A How Nebuchadnaser, of biblical history fell from grace to grass, so has Kwame Nkrumah who thought that he was mightier than God has fallen from self-created grace to grass. The myth which he created to surround himself has been broken by the Ghana Armed Forces and the Police on February 24. No doubt, Kwame Nkrumah will die a pauper.

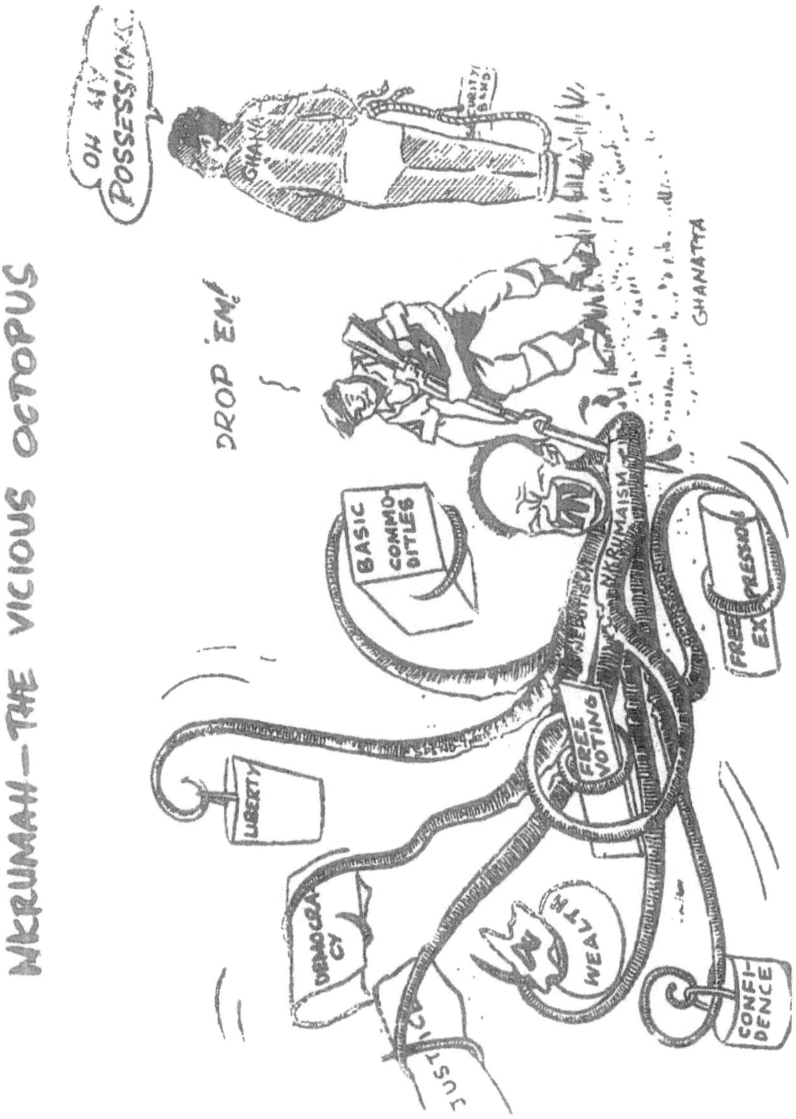

Post-coup Cartoons 81

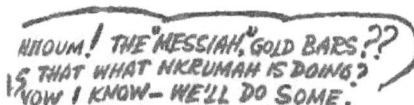

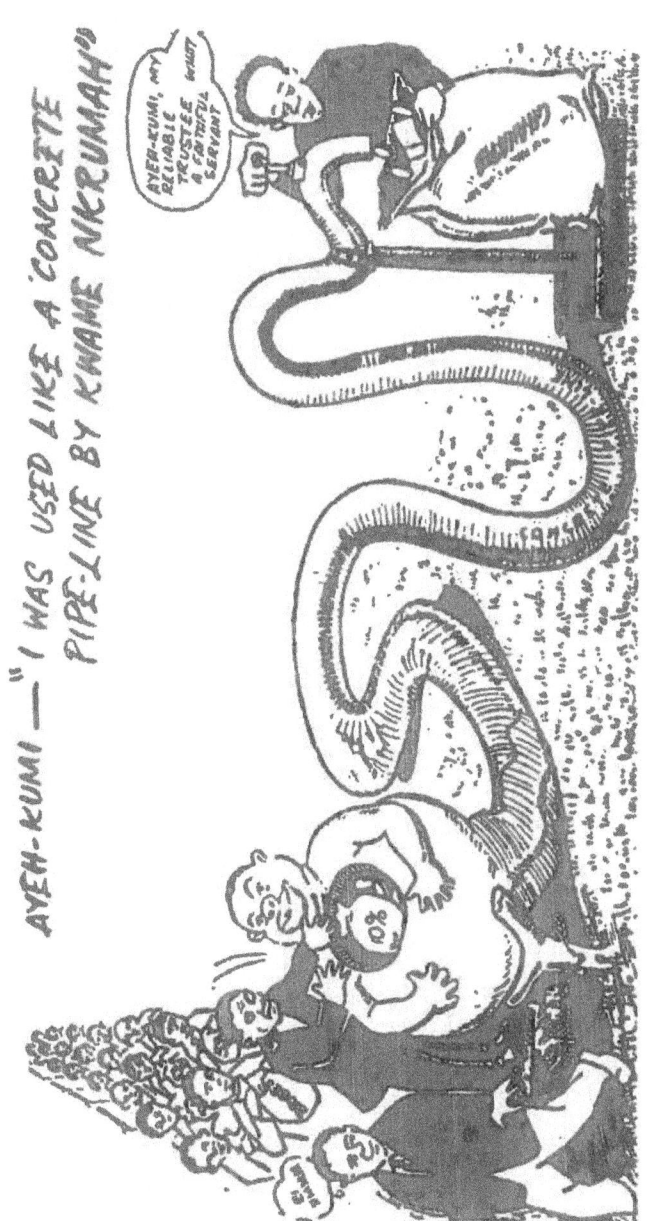

Post-coup Cartoons

Post-coup Cartoons

KWAKU-BOATENG — THE GAPING SYCOPHANT

...AND BONFIRE WAS MADE OF THE TREASURED BOOKS OF NKRUMAISM.

SOME OF THESE WOMEN STOOPED TOO LOW FOR HELP.
YOU KNOW MY HUSBAND IS DEAD AND I NEED YOUR HELP IN ALL RESPECTS. IS THAT THOUSAND POUNDS? YIE, ADD FIVE HUN-DRED MORE! OH, KWAME, MY BENE-FACTOR...
YOU DON'T HAVE TO WORRY. YOUR TROUBLES WILL BE TAKEN CARE OF. DO YOU SAY £500 MORE? O.K THAT MAKES IT £1,500.
STATE FUNDS

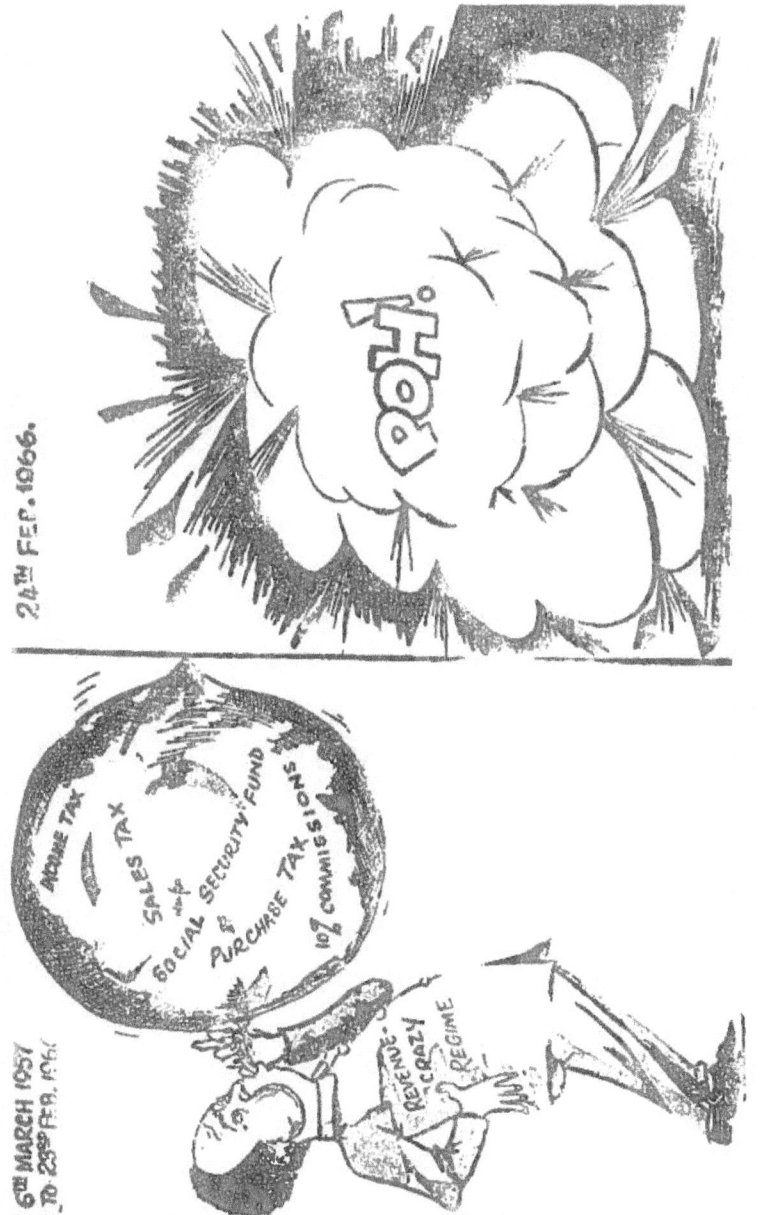

We have always taken the stand that Sekon Toure of Guinea is nursing a venomous serpent in his bosom. Why he gives Nkrumah the chance to rant on his country's radio against Ghana only he and his Kankan Nyame knows.

If the goofy deposed president says he is coming, let him ... We are here, waiting !

www.ingramcontent.com/pod-product-compliance
Lightning Source LLC
Chambersburg PA
CBHW060420300426
44111CB00018B/2918